GET IT DESIGNED!

Build the Business of Your Dreams

"Where there is no vision, the people perish."
Proverbs 29:18

Table of Contents

GET IT DESIGNED!
Build the Business of Your Dreams

"What do they have that I don't?"

As an entrepreneur or woman in business, have you asked yourself that question?

It's easy to look around and suffer from the "compare and despair" syndrome, in a world that is so connected that we all know what everyone else does - or at least what they (or other people) want us to know about what they do in their lives. Social media posts give the perception that others have all of the answers when it comes to running and growing a successful business. If you dig a little deeper than the social media surface, however, you will find that most of us have the same questions, concerns, and needs. And none of us are perfect!

Evidence shows that reaching out to other people can fast-forward your business growth. Networking is a wonderful way to reach out to others, create relationships, and share knowledge. Mastermind groups are also very popular for a good reason. They enable a group of people in business to brainstorm, learn, hold each other accountable, and provide support to hone their business and personal skills. Their goal is for all of the members of the group to succeed.

Conferences such as the Business Resources for Inspiring Leaders, or BRIL Conference, also encourage and engage business women from different fields of expertise but with similar challenges with entrepreneurship and corporate environments to share what they know.

We want you to change your mindset. Better than asking, **"What do they have that I don't?"** is inquiring, **"What specifically do I**

1

need to take my business to the next level?" While they are all subject matter experts, the authors of this BRIL book have been in your shoes and they have come together in the following pages to share their wisdom and experiences with you. Remember: "You don't have enough time or enough money to learn everything through your own experience. You'd better learn to listen," as a friend of mine would say. Here is your opportunity to learn that:

- ➢ Networking is a big part of how the BRIL speakers and participants have grown their businesses. They have figured out how to make the connections that are crucial to their success. **Bettina Mason** shares how to not only connect with others but to be a servant leader in your community to scale your business to the size you envision.

- ➢ Communication is essential for making good decisions, connecting with others, and sharing your business vision. **Diana Parra, M.A.,** expertly dissects three essential ways that will massively improve your communication with others.

- ➢ The true value of a product lies not within the item itself but instead resides in what the customer deems worthy about the item. **Denali Roberts** has a refreshing take on marketing to give you a whole new formula for promoting your business.

- ➢ Once you understand the value potential clients place on products, the next step in marketing is understanding why people buy and which features attract them to make the sale. **Malee Ouja** shares fascinating insights about the new psychology of marketing.

- ➢ LinkedIn is more than just "Facebook for Business"...it's a tool to take your business to the next level. **Cheryl Matt** understands how LinkedIn is a powerful business-building tool for attracting more leads and clients. Learn her insightful tips on how to use LinkedIn for your business.

➢ How often do you step away from the day-to-day details of your work life and really look at *why* you are doing what you do? If you haven't thought about this in a while, it's time to take a look at your purpose. **Teri Karjala** examines living life with intention so we can create more – especially more of what we *really* want – with less effort and more satisfaction.

➢ When examining your life's purpose, have you discovered that you have a side hustle you would like to turn into a full-time business? **Dr. Shantell Malachi** reveals how taking a chance on a passion catapulted her into her dream job. She accomplished this through vision and followed it up with work to make her dream come true.

➢ In business it takes money to fuel your success. **Sorana Blackfoot** shares budgeting tips for the unbudgetable so you can not only achieve your mission for your business but also become profitable.

➢ Potential clients aren't just buying your products or services; potential clients are buying *you* – your brand, what you believe in, and what makes you stand out. Writing a regularly posted blog is a great way to share more about you as a person so your potential and current clients feel they have a relationship with you. **Kim Eley** shares five powerful ways that writing your blog can improve your business.

➢ Have you ever said to yourself, "There's just no hope. I can't do this." We want to introduce you to a woman who teaches through her daily life that there are no excuses for this kind of thinking. **Tawana Williams** lived a life that would cause many of us to despair. She has turned a disability into a superpower to inspire, uplift, and permanently change minds about what is possible.

Building Ultimate Relationships
Bettina Mason

"Do unto others as you would have them do unto you."
Matthew 7:12

Meeting people and engaging in conversation is one of my passions, especially when I can talk about collaboration efforts for our community. It is my purpose to be a servant leader. In order to meet the needs of our community and beyond, one must collaborate with as many people as possible to aid in these efforts; it is definitely more productive.

I have never met a stranger, meaning I will talk to anyone without any problems. I delight in meeting new people; it comes naturally to me. Going into a room energizes me and I gravitate towards like-minded people, specifically people who want to work together towards a common goal.

The purpose of my current job as a Community Outreach Specialist is to connect with people as well as building community partnerships. I strategically choose events where I can meet as many people as possible. The thrill of meeting new people, learning more about their business, making connections, creating new strategic alliances, and helping the people in our Virginia communities is an outstanding feeling!

Business relationships have been a beneficial part of my life in both my career as well as business endeavors; "It is not what you know, but who you know!" After looking for a job for over a year, using job sites, and online advertisements, it was a business relationship that afforded me my next career opportunity. We need to focus our efforts on the network of positive relationships we have forged on our journey; it will help us with further aspects of our business lives. Connections are paramount!

Relationships are the foundation of success! People will always do business with people they know, like, and trust. No matter what we experience in our lifetime, we need to forge a pathway to success by fostering trust through partnerships/strategic alliances for effective future endeavors. While individuals are talented, it would be more beneficial to work with others collectively towards a mutual goal as well as build upon that trust.

Building better relationships can be rewarding; however, the time for this cultivation will vary from person to person. It is important to realize that relationships are powerful, and they can be lucrative for their duration. Here are some helpful hints to aid in the quest in building ultimate relationships in your lifetime!

Networking

Identify your areas of interest, who you want to meet, and above all, what you want to accomplish by building any specific relationship. Be intentional and stay focused on your goals. Choose events, locations, meetings, associations, business groups, and organizations that can give you an advantageous position when meeting potential partners. Make sure your introduction is clear and concise; i.e., share your name, company, title, and brief description of what you do currently in your life. Know your value proposition! Engagement is imperative; it can ensure future conversations. Capture their attention, establish a rapport, and move to the next level which will be to follow up and eventually even work together! Don't be shy!

Hint:

- ***Do*** *scale back and focus on your conversation; too much information at the first meeting can be overwhelming.*

- **Do** have your business cards available, regardless if you have a full-time job. It is important to have pertinent contact information on hand immediately. Your information should consist of name, number, email, title, or area of interest.

- **Don't** be pushy.

- **Don't** gossip, as you can easily lose your credibility because your focus has shifted to something that is not important to obtaining this partnership; it is a distraction.

Listening

Active listening skills will allow a better understanding of the person you are meeting. It also establishes rapport, sets the tone, and makes them feel important, thus always listen more than you talk. As the old saying goes, "you have two ears and one mouth for a reason." The ability to listen intently will give you the opportunity to ask probing questions and get the clarification needed to move forward or not. What can this person bring to this partnership? Make sure to be attentive, ask for clarification, give appropriate feedback, and ask for a follow up meeting, if applicable. This will give you the opportunity to learn more information about your potential partner.

Hint:

- **Do** lean in and make eye-to-eye contact during the conversation to show genuine interest (non-verbal clues). Make them feel like they are the only one in the room.

- **Don't** allow distractions to invade your ability to listen carefully; i.e., taking a phone call, speaking with someone else as they are passing, not keeping eye *contact, or looking around the room instead of paying attention to them.*

Connections

Your initial meeting is not only to discuss business, but to discover the connections which would make a successful partnership. The conversation should be organic and authentic, not rehearsed or robotic. Find out your commonalities during your conversation which will help in the discovery of a kindred spirit!

As the relationship progresses, use these connections to solidify this foundation. Make sure you focus on the quality more than the quantity of connections you can make.

Hint:
- ***Do** use your five senses - taste, touch, sight, smell, and hearing - to look for clues to make a connection in any way possible. Use these clues to keep the conversation interesting as well as initializing the trust needed to work together.*

   - *For example, if you notice a college ring on the finger of the person you are meeting, find a connection to that school. Perhaps you or someone you know attended that school, thus making it a great conversation starter.*

- ***Do** find anything that will aid you with a great conversation with flow and connectivity.*

- ***Don't** take advantage of your new connection by immediately asking them for favors, products, or other's information before you can make a real connection with this person.*

- **Do** concentrate on growing this possible new relationship.

Mindfulness

> *Stay present for the 'now' of your life.*
> *It's your point of power.*
> *-Doug Dillion*

Always be mindful or aware of your surroundings, the audience, and especially the conversation with your future partner. Remember the reason why you are pursuing the partnership and focus on sharing information that will foster solid relationships. Live in the moment and do not get ahead of yourself assuming this will be an ideal relationship.

Follow the Golden Rule: **"Treat people like you want to be treated."** Emotions play a huge role in working with others. Learn how to recognize their idiosyncrasies and use them to your advantage when diversifying efforts and finding a variety of solutions.

Hint:

- **Do** *go with the flow and move fluidly through this process.*

- **Don't** *feel like every new meeting is going to be the business relationship of your dreams. These initial meetings may be just a meeting at an event. If so, keep moving. Do not try to force any relationship; it needs to be organic.*

Respect

Respect the space and time of your potential partner. Do not overpower the conversation and usurp all of the person's time by rambling about information that does not pertain to the overall goal. Contact the partner to set up another meeting and do not show up at their office without an appointment; manage your boundaries. Continue to stay positive and never exude negativity via actions or words. The goal is to build a strong foundation in order to meet the needs of all shareholders.

Hint:

- **Do** *follow the "Golden Rule." Treat people like you want to be treated.*

- **Do** *adhere to the appropriate interpersonal space while communicating; i.e., social distance (5-12 feet). When you get into someone's personal space (2-4 feet), it becomes invasive and intimidating.*

- **Don't** *speak as if you are too familiar upon your first meeting; keep it related to business.*

- **Don't** *waste anyone's time if the meeting is not what you were hoping for at the time. If you are not a good fit for each other then move on to the next opportunity.*

Be Yourself

You are an original! What you bring to the table is important and your ability to work with others is paramount. Some people may have difficulties being able to have a basic conversation with strangers, but once they start talking to people and finding common ground, it will become easier; practice makes perfect. If you are passionate about what you are wanting to achieve in your business and your community, the message will ring loud and clear to those who want the same thing. Presenting a "false self" can easily be perceived as being untrustworthy, which can be detrimental to your initial meeting; trust is key!

Hint:

- **Do** *stay true to yourself, and above all be yourself! People can recognize a fake, so keep it real.*

- **Do** *be positive.*

- **Don't** *bring any negative vibes into this relationship from bad experiences in your past.*

- **Don't** *be braggadocios; hone it in and be humble.*

Follow-Up

It is important to follow up with your potential business partners. The fortune is in the follow-up! The point of meeting people and building relationships is to continue the conversation on a consistent basis.

Hint:

- **Do** *be consistent and collaborative. Be willing to work well with others, like in kindergarten.*

- **Do** *be reliable.*

- **Don't** *take too long to follow up.*

- **Don't** *make promises that you cannot keep.*

Relationships need to evolve over time and will not happen at the first meeting. Start building by establishing a solid foundation of mutual trust while consistently working together to meet a shared goal. Collaborative efforts are also an effective way to reach shared initiatives successfully.

It is imperative that one realizes the importance of building relationships. You are not in this alone and if you can meet the right people then capitalize on those opportunities. Recognize the importance of investing in the work/business relationships because they will become long-term generators of business!

Bettina Mason

Bettina Mason is the principal/founder of Mason Education Solutions Group, LLC., and the creator of the 3C Process-Leadership Development Training. She currently works as an Outreach Specialist for a Fortune 500 insurance company. She is a trainer, facilitator, and educator by trade, with a passion for building ultimate relationships while connecting people with community resources that can provide a better quality of life or better business opportunities.

An experienced Human Resources leader (over 25 years) with a demonstrated history of working in training and development within various companies, Bettina has worked with both small and large businesses and in both higher and secondary education arenas. She is a high-energy professional with a B.A in Communications/Public Relations and an MSEd. focused in Training and Development from James Madison University. She is a Society for Human Resources Certified Professional (SHRM-CP).

Contact Info:

Email: bettmason@gmail.com

Phone: (540) 915-2689

Social Media: @BettinaMason Edu

Three Essential Keys to Communication That Will Massively Improve the Way You Communicate with Others

Diana Parra, M.A.

Communication is key in everything we do. Every interaction is influenced by communication. This interaction can be positive or negative, and communication can be verbal or non-verbal. This is why it is so important to make sure we are communicating effectively. If we want to get our point across, we need to be able to hear others' points of view as well. In other words, if we desire to be heard, we must start by listening to others.

The problem is that most of us don't know how to communicate. This is not our fault. We are not taught this skill as kids by our parents or in school. Early on, we are taught that if we want something we should "use our words" or "work it out" with the other person. But what does that really mean? What does that look like? I believe that for the most part, as young children, we are implicitly taught to focus on fulfilling our needs and desires without taking into account those of others. But most importantly, we are not taught how to communicate in a manner that fosters cooperation and collaboration.

Poor communication can have negative results, not just in your professional life but also in your personal life. It can lead to arguments, with people feeling resentful, frustrated, and overwhelmed, thereby damaging relationships. It can also lead to failed projects, unmet deadlines, procrastination, and blaming others.

Furthermore, as women we are taught to "listen" rather than express how we feel. Sometimes this translates (professionally and personally) into wanting to please others at the expense of our own needs and desires. We silence ourselves and stifle our voices for fear of "upsetting" someone or being perceived as "controlling" or "masculine."

Whether you are a woman or a man, effective leadership requires effective communication. As a leader, you have to know how to get your vision and message across clearly; how to affect change and inspire; and how to foster creativity, collaboration and healthy relationships. You, as a leader, set the example and the tone for the rest of the organization.

The Three Keys

Key #1: Clarity

Before you engage with anyone, you have to be super clear on three things: who, what, and how.

Who is your audience?

Who is the communication with? Is it with your boss, team members, peers, or clients? Your relationship with each one of these people is very different. You would not approach your boss the same way you approach a client or customer, right? You might be more informal with your peers than with your boss and clients.

What is it you want to communicate?

What is the purpose of the communication? What is the message you want to get across? You want to think in terms of outcome. What is the ultimate outcome you are seeking? Is it meeting a deadline? Is it a promotion? Is it resolution to a problem? What do you want to happen?

How will you deliver the communication?

How will you deliver the message? Here you want to be mindful of two things: Medium and Tone.

Medium

What medium are you using to communicate? Is it face-to-face? Via email or text? Is it a teleconference? These are all different methods and require different approaches. If you are speaking with someone face-to-face, you have a lot more information to process which helps you discern which way the conversation is going and how you need to proceed. If you are having an exchange over email or text, you lose a lot of the intricacies, such as body language, facial expressions and tone. This is why so many miscommunications happen in this medium.

Tone

What is the tone you are using with the other person? What is theirs? This is easier when you have a face-to-face exchange. That's because you are better able to read the other person's tone and respond accordingly. You can also be aware of yours and adjust it as well. For example, if you notice yourself getting frustrated and your tone starts to show it, you will want to adjust it to keep the conversation open. If you notice the other person getting frustrated, you can address it by acknowledging it and asking what they need in that moment to keep the conversation moving in a positive direction.

The same applies when you are communicating over email or text. If you are not sure of the tone in the email or text, you can ask a question such as: "I sense some frustration in your text/email; is this correct? Is there something I can do?" Too often, we don't ask and we simply assume. This leads to breakdown in communication.

When you have **Clarity** about the Who, What, and How, the other person will feel understood. You see, most people focus solely on what they want and don't take the time to get to know or understand the other person. When we are clear on the Who, What, and How, we have taken the time to understand the other person even if it's just a little. We are being mindful of the fact that we are engaging in an exchange with another person, not a "title" or "role." In other words, we are communicating with a human being, not a "boss" or "peer."

If you are not super clear on the Who, What, and How, chances are you will not get the results you are seeking.

Key #2: Active Listening

Active listening is the Master Key to effective communication. That's because we are all seeking to be heard. Feeling heard makes us feel understood, and what every person (no matter their role or title) wants most is to feel heard and understood.

The problem is that most people "hear" what the other person is saying but they don't really "listen." We get caught up in thinking how to respond or defend our point which distracts us from truly listening and understanding what the other person is saying. Active listening enables us to form meaningful relationships and connections. In the workplace, this translates to cohesion and trust. Active listening is a learned skill, and it requires time and much practice.

Here are two techniques to get you started practicing active listening:

1. Pay attention:
   - Make and maintain eye contact.
   - Put away all distractions (phone, computer, etc.).
   - Practice focusing on the here and now of the conversation and avoid distracting thoughts.
   - Listen to everything the other person has to say first before thinking about what you are going to say next and how you are going to respond. This way you avoid being distracted from what the other person is saying.

2. Provide feedback:
   - Ask for questions for clarification (e.g. "What do you mean?" "Is this what you mean?" "Tell me more...")
   - Paraphrase to reflect back that you are listening (e.g. "what I hear you saying is..." "It sounds like you are saying...")
   - Don't interrupt. This frustrates the speaker and can limit how the message is understood. Instead, allow the speaker to finish each point before asking questions and don't interrupt with counter points.

When you practice active listening you can stay focused on the other person, truly listen, and understand their point of view. You are then more likely to engage in a mutually respectful way and hear their point of view, and have yours heard as well.

Key #3: Action

Action means you approach the conversation with the understanding that you will be action- and solution-oriented. Be prepared. What does this mean? It means that before you engage in a conversation to resolve a problem or challenge, you will have thought about possible solutions. Your communication should state the problem or challenge but should not be focused on it. The focus should be on the solution.

There are three steps here:

1. Propose a possible solution to the problem or offer to brainstorm together.

2. Offer to do something towards the solution (What can I do, say, provide, be in charge of?). Adopt a *"Let's work together"* attitude.

3. Follow through. This is an important step because it builds trust. People who don't follow through are rarely trusted. They are perceived as unreliable, and in a team situation, are seen as letting their team down. If you say you are going to do something, **DO IT!**

Taking action and following these three simple steps builds trust, and people who are trusted are more likely to influence others. This is extremely important in the workplace because it will foster collaboration and teamwork, which in turn can lead to a successful outcome.

Diana Parra, M.A.
Founder and CEO
Akros Leadership International, LLC
Coach, Author & Speaker

Diana Parra, M.A. is a leadership coach and transformational strategist for women entrepreneurs and professional women, a high-performance coach for female executives, a speaker, and an author.

She is the founder and CEO of Akros Leadership International, a leadership development company whose mission is to create a community of leaders dedicated to empowering and inspiring others by leading with love and compassion, while elevating the world at large.

Her 20 plus years of combined experience as a manager, therapist, coach, and consultant have forged in her a unique approach to leadership development. She holds a Bachelor's degree in Psychology from Rutgers University and a Master's degree in Educational Psychology with a concentration in Clinical Psychology from Montclair State University. Diana has also completed doctoral level coursework in Organizational Psychology at the Rutgers University Graduate School of Applied and Professional Psychology and is a graduate of Anthony Robbins Business Mastery and Anthony Robbins Mastery University.

Diana is coauthor of *Get It Done: Design the Business of Your Dreams* and has recently published her own book: *Leading with a Broken Heart: Finding Gold in Our Darkest Moments*.

Diana was born in Colombia and is bilingual and bi-cultural. She is married with three adoptive children. She loves to explore the world, personal-development, music, yoga, and nature.

Contact Info:

Website: www.akrosinternational.com

Email: Diana@akrosinternational.com

Phone: 804-286-2426

Bring on the Whiskey and Pass the Marketing!
Denali Roberts

As I sat down with a long-time friend at a local bar, the bartender walked over, turned to my friend, and said, "Good evening ma'am, what can I get you to drink?"

She replied, "A Miller Light, please."

He slid a coaster to her and turned to me and said, "And for you ma'am?"

I replied, "I would love an Old Fashioned, please."

He nodded and replied, "Do you have a preference in whiskey?"

"Which is the best?" I responded.

"I don't know ma'am; they all taste the same to me."

I was puzzled and confused about how a bartender didn't have a favorite whiskey. How did he not know which one is the best?

I cocked my head and finally replied, "I'll take whatever you usually make it with."

Admittedly, I was even more confused at this point. Why did I not give him my preference of whiskey? Do I not have a preference?

I thought about this conversation for days. Looking at it from a marketing point of view, this conversation was astonishing. Companies spend millions of dollars a year on their marketing campaigns, running elaborate TV ads, promoting via social media, buying radio ads, sponsoring events, and having influencers who promote them and all these tactics target their audience in hopes they will decide to purchase from them. Companies spend a considerable amount of time on their marketing, attracting new customers, and retaining the customer base they currently have, and yet, here I was with no preference in the whiskey I ordered.

So, where did the bartender and I go wrong? After thinking it over, my answer lies in this: all the products we see and buy are versions of other products. Products might have slight differences in packaging for a different experience. Some are more advanced; others are better made. Companies spend millions of dollars a year on marketing campaigns because it's not about the product, it's about the value that the customer places on that product. A company who places a higher value on their marketing and their customers believe that the product has a high value will see an increase in sales and an increase in demand for the product.

Let's take the case of the retail industry. Each season we need new clothes to keep us cool or warm. We typically don't want to spend a fortune on clothing; however, we have numerous expensive retailers. We could go to Wal-Mart to get our clothing and instead we go to Nordstrom. But why?

The answer is that we associate a value for each of these retailers. We value how they make us feel. We value how accessible they are and we value how many comments we get on our clothing. The value we associate with each of these companies is what will be the deciding factor when we go to make a transaction. Value can be explained as:

Value = Preferences + Product + Perception

Our preference is the product we are looking for, the product is how accessible it is to us, and the perception is how we look and feel about the product. Therefore, we choose to shop at Nordstrom over Wal-Mart because we may find the clothing we are looking for, it might be more easily accessible to us, and we may love how we feel wearing the quality clothing. The opportunity for a product to receive a value from a customer is when a company places a high importance on their marketing.

A customer cares about the value and the company cares about the marketing, which gives the customer an idea of the value they bring. A company's primary goal is to market their business to their target audience in order for sales to be made. When a company creates a highly refined and effective marketing campaign, they are better able to market to their customers and to show them the value that they offer in order for customers to choose their product over another.

Let's go back to the night at the bar. There was no preference of whiskey because neither of us placed a value on one whiskey over another. The taste wasn't better and neither whiskey stood out. We both fell victim because we didn't know which one had a higher value. The whiskey companies have to be bold enough to stand apart and ensure that the bartender and I remember not only which company is our favorite but also pack enough value into their marketing that we find them the best. Being the best is a game of marketing and the same goes for why we didn't have a preference in whiskey. We didn't value one of them as the best, however, whiskey companies could win this game very easily.

After analyzing the idea that companies market themselves to portray a value to the customer, it is evident that companies who lack in marketing, lack in having a value, thus, they have lower sales and few customers. Imagine what would happen if a company of any size decided to pour several hundred dollars a year into their marketing, or heck, even a few thousand dollars into their marketing? The impact it would make for that company would be huge.

Let's think back to our value formula. The more you market your company, the more product you sell, thus having a well-known perception. With more product out and a well-known perception, your company will find itself with more sales and more returning customers, all because of your marketing.

Companies who place a higher importance on their marketing by having an advanced range of marketing tactics and a highly refined campaign that has both value and that sets them apart will find their business grows faster and stronger, for longer. Marketing is a pinnacle aspect of your company; to not market your business is saying you don't want sales. Your company should have a marketing campaign that is tailored to your target audience, in all tactics you take, and should bring in the perfect customer for you. Marketing will set you apart. Marketing will make you the best. Create value in order for your customer to enjoy the product you offer. Be the company that I remember to order and the bartender remembers to recommend.

Denali Roberts

Denali Roberts is a serial entrepreneur, author, marketing strategist and speaker. She started her first business at the age of 12 and another at 17 years old. While finishing her high school education, Denali was the COO of Mabel's Espresso Bakery Cafe, the family business. It was at Mabel's that she honed her business-savvy senses by increasing profit margins and performance exponentially, formulating effective protocols, and streamlining processes. Denali is an undergraduate student at the University of Mary Washington where she actively works with the local business and the Center for Economic Development at UMW. She believes strongly that all people, including students, should take risks with entrepreneurship and live the life they always wanted. She will graduate in May 2020.

Pendleton Works (PW) was founded in January of 2018. Denali serves as the CEO & Founder. PW shows business owners how to use marketing to enhance their visibility and increase their ROI. Pendleton Works is a full-service marketing firm that offers web design, social media marketing, branding, graphic design, marketing strategy and development, training, and much more. Denali also serves as Co-Founder of Jade Skin Care. Jade Skin Care is a multi-level marketing company that brings customized skin care solutions to women of all races, ethnicities, and backgrounds by using Korean Beauty products. She has plans already in place to incorporate her passion and appreciation for global cultures into her business model. Working in this field and helping others to improve in their business ventures is Denali Roberts' heart and soul, and she loves being able to share it with her family, clients, and community.

Contact Info:

Website: www.pendletonworks.com

Email: droberts@pendletonworks.com

Phone: 804-517-6361

Social Media: @pendletonworks

The New Psychology of Marketing
Malee Ojua

Owning and running a small business is tougher now than ever before. In an age where consumers are growing skeptical and resistant to traditional sales techniques, and when competition is fierce, it can be difficult to stand out. How can buyers hear you and your story when there is so much noise and competition in the market? How can you grow your business and find the right system to put in place in a market that is so crowded, fast-paced, and often unforgiving?

The answer is a simple yet overlooked one. It is about getting into the right mindset — and understanding the new psychology of marketing.

The Psychology of Marketing

What drives a customer to buy and what draws their attention? Human beings have a built-in response to stimuli. These behaviors are called fixed action patterns. They are instinctive, innate behaviors. The measure of these responses taken when a customer observes an advertisement is called neuromarketing.

Neuromarketing is a process. If you struggle to figure out the right systems to put in place for your business, want to take your business to the next level, grow sales, or become a recognized contributor in your community, you need to use neuromarketing to tap into the minds of your customers so that they are triggered to buy your product. You can use neuromarketing by:

1. Using the power of persuasion and understanding the reptilian brain

2. Recognizing your customers' pain points

29

3. Demonstrating how your product is different and how it has value over your competitors' products

4. Demonstrating how your product helps people and why consumers need it

The Power of Persuasion

The psychology of persuasion is the ability to persuade or influence a person to act using certain principles which play into our innate behaviors and beliefs. People are trying to influence others (and you) all of the time. In sales and business, it is often done in a very subtle way. Persuasion can influence a person's action, behaviors, attitudes, and beliefs. It is a tool that is used commonly in business for personal gain and sales.

So how can this help you and your business? By using the concepts of the power of persuasion and neuromarketing, you can tap into the minds of your consumers and achieve the success you desire.

Robert Cialdini, author of *Influence: The Psychology of Persuasion*, states that there are six principles of persuasion:

1. Reciprocity
2. Scarcity
3. Authority
4. Consistency
5. Liking
6. Consensus

These universal principles of persuasion which guide human behavior are all practical, effective, and costless. By understanding and using these principles in a business setting, you can achieve your goals, improve sales, and increase conversion rates.

The Reptilian Brain

The reptilian brain is our gatekeeper and decision maker. It is the oldest part of our brain and is responsible for our survival instincts. It focuses primarily on pain. Marketers can grab the reptilian brain's attention by addressing a pain point that a consumer is experiencing. By identifying your customer's pain points, you can use your power of persuasion to explain how you can solve their issues.

How to Address the Pain Points

Successful marketing makes consumers curious about how a product helps them. What does your customer need? What is the problem they are facing, and how can you provide them with a solution to that problem?

To grow your business and get consumers to buy your product or service, you have to recognize their **pain point**. This is what will differentiate yourself and your brand.

Put yourself in the shoes of your target audience. Experience the pain they are experiencing. Take a moment to focus on the chair you are sitting in, the paper you are reading, and the shirt you are wearing. Why was that product created? What pain point does it satisfy?

Consider this: Have you ever ordered UberEats? The UberEats service addresses a vital pain point: the pain of having to leave the comfort of your own home to get food. The solution? Ordering from the comfort of your own home, from a huge selection of restaurants — without having to worry about taking out cash. There's a reason UberEats is now the fastest growing meal delivery service in U.S. history!

In my business, my clients want more clients. They want revenue and profit. The truth is, most clients won't say that. They will say that they want to have more of an impact and make a bigger difference, but the truth of the matter is that they want it all. To find a way to help my clients achieve their goals, I have to differentiate myself from my competitors.

Our brains filter whether we're open to deciding to buy or not by responding to certain criteria that address these pain points and patterns:

1. What's in It for Me?

How is your product different? How does it help people? A consumer's reptilian brain is self-centered in nature. Consumers are more likely to be drawn to a product or service that gives them value.

For example, when I was an aerospace engineer, I was able to market multi-billion-dollar satellite systems for defense to *hundreds* of military generals at a time. Why was I able to do this?

I marketed to them successfully because I understood they only cared about and needed to know two things:

1. Would the satellite work the way I said it would, and
2. Would their men come home safely?

You have to tap into a consumer's selfish side and appeal to the reptilian brain's self-centered nature. Give your customer what they need. Tell them how you can help them and how you can provide a solution to their pain point.

2. Disruption or Changes

Another pain point for our clients is a disruption or change. Our reptilian brains are wired to react to changes in our lives as a threat, prompting us to want to fight or run away. Disruptions are necessary to bypass this fight or flight autonomic response. Tell a story, use simple language. Do what you can to disrupt your customer's normal pattern of thinking.

In marketing, a pattern interrupt surprises consumers. It breaks their normal thinking pattern and grabs their attention. It engages them, keeps boredom at bay, encourages them to take action, and helps you position your product or brand. For example, if you are promoting a product or service in a video, a pattern interrupt could be a pop-up poll or question that makes viewers snap back into paying attention. It also engages them. There are all sorts of different pattern interrupts you can use in your marketing materials to stimulate this type of response.

Interrupt Your Own Pattern

Stand up right now. Put down your phone. Ignore whatever is in front of you. Walk around and clear your mind.

- What is it exactly that sets your product or service apart from your competitors?
- How can you communicate these differences in a simple way?
- How can you communicate these differences in a way that interrupts a consumer's normal thinking patterns?
- How can you use disruption and change in your own way of thinking to grow your business and be recognized for your contribution to your community?

My own experience with disruption and interruption is what led me to where I am today. I am the owner of a successful, multiple six-figure marketing agency. I began my career as an engineer, but after a pivotal moment in my life, I decided to make a change. I wanted to do something about which I was passionate.

I wanted to make a difference — but I also wanted to make money. I made a major change in my life and out of it came my booming business, Sacred Fire Creative. Today, my business focuses on working with women and minority business owners, but I have also worked with big corporations like NYU Hospital and Johnson & Johnson. I work with service-based professionals and experts who want to grow an authentic brand that captures hearts and converts customers. I made a major change in my life which led me to where I am today.

Focus on making disruptions and changes in your life, your career, and the way you market to consumers. Your business will reap the rewards.

3. The Beginning and the End

The brain directs most of its attention to the beginnings and ends of marketing materials. Use this by focusing on sending the main points of your message at the beginning and repeating them at the end. Another method is to introduce a pattern interrupt, which creates a new beginning and breaks the pattern of thought by grabbing a consumer's attention.

4. Keep it Simple

Is your product or service familiar? Friendly? Or is it something that is complex? Make your product simple — even if it isn't — and avoid complex concepts. Make it something a consumer will understand.

5. Visual Imagery

Human beings are visual creatures! Visual decision making allows brands to attract and engage people to take action using images. Successful marketing uses brand images and techniques in visual advertising to select images that represent an organization and brand.

To capitalize on visual decision making, you need to leverage visual content in marketing materials. Show your customer what your product will deliver and make the message simple.

6. Emotion

"I've learned that people will forget what you said, people will forget what you did, but people will never forget how you made them feel." - Maya Angelou.

Emotions make up the foundation of how decisions are made, and today most consumers are drawn towards marketing content that is warm, inspires them, and makes them feel something. You need to make your clients feel inspired. Learn how to focus on core human emotions in advertising, and use this emotion to drive connections and awareness.

How to Stand Apart

So what are my differentiators?

My differentiators are spiritual mixed with analytical. I bridge the gap between the functional, logical brain and the creative, imaginative right brain. This is what sets my business apart from my competitors.

Finding the Right Solution for Your Customers

Your business has to overcome your customers' pain points. It has to deliver a solution to the reptilian brain. To find the right solution for your customers, use the principles of persuasion to influence a consumer to take action while appealing to their reptilian brain:

- Demonstrate value through contrast
- Appeal to the emotions of your customers
- Use visual imagery: show a visual representation of your product
- Consider pattern interrupts
- Tell an emotional story that helps consumers understand how you can help them
- Appeal to the reptilian brain's self-centered nature to influence your audience
- Identify your audience's pain points, and tell them how you can fix that pain

What Is *Your* Pain Point?

Think about *your* pain points. What pain are you experiencing? Are you experiencing the pain of not knowing how to grow your business? Are you worrying about how you will pay your bills? Well, there is a solution to this.

Imagine a world without this pain, and one beyond that. Think of my story: going from a broke energy healer on food stamps to an owner of a multi-six-figure digital marketing agency working with world-renowned companies like Johnson & Johnson.

Growing your business and your brain doesn't have to be complicated. You just have to understand how the psychology of marketing works, and use this knowledge to tap into a consumer's primitive, innate instincts while giving them a solution to a problem they experience every day.

Malee Ojua

Malee Ojua, CEO & Digital Marketing Strategist of Sacred Fire Creative, helps change makers, service-based professionals, and experts who want to grow an authentic brand that captures hearts and converts more customers through her Lucrative Brand Blueprint. Through Sacred Fire Creative, she guides visionary women and minority leaders as they leave their legacy and connect with their tribe through branding, web design, and marketing.

Malee earned her degree in Web Development and Design, as well as Master's degrees in Public Policy and Aerospace Engineering from the Massachusetts Institute of Technology. Her corporate experience involved Top Secret government clearance to create future generations of satellite systems. Malee has also served on the faculty of Portland Community College's Web Design & Development Department, teaching Search Engine Optimization and Wordpress.

Her web design and marketing clients take comfort in knowing that they have a rocket scientist on their team who's ready to solve their most pressing design and marketing problems. Malee works with socially conscious entrepreneurs who are ready to make a greater positive impact on their community and the world.

Contact Info:

Website: www.sacredfirecreative.com

Phone: 503-816-3890

Facebook: https://www.facebook.com/sacredfirecreative/

LinkedIn: https://www.linkedin.com/company/sacred-fire-creative/

Twitter: https://twitter.com/sacred_fire_pdx

Instagram: https://www.instagram.com/sacred_fire_creative/

Pinterest: https://in.pinterest.com/sacred_fire/

YouTube: https://www.youtube.com/user/sacredfirecreative/

Leveraging LinkedIn For Business Growth
Cheryl Matt

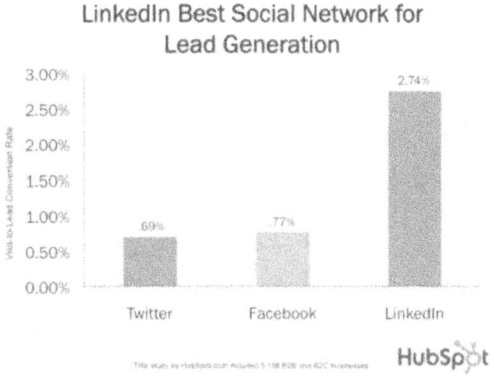

With over 550,000 million users worldwide and two new members joining every second, LinkedIn is not just another social network. LinkedIn is a powerful business-building tool for attracting more leads and clients. According to a survey conducted by Hubspot Survey, this lead generating goldmine is over 277% more effective for lead generation than any other social media platform.

Following are a few more statistics that might compel you to incorporate LinkedIn into your marketing plan:

- Over 80% of all business to business (B2B) leads generated by social media come from LinkedIn. (Source: LinkedIn)

- 90% of top performing sales people now use social media as part of their sales strategy. (Source: LinkedIn State of Sales Report)

- 79% of B2B Marketers say LinkedIn is an effective source for generating leads. (Source: LinkedIn)

LinkedIn is the perfect source for inbound and outbound marketing.

Inbound Marketing

Linkedin is a great tool for inbound marketing (drawing customers to your products or services via content marketing, social media marketing, search engine optimization and branding). Your LinkedIn profile is available 24 hours a day, 7 days a week to your prospects. Having a LinkedIn Profile is like having another business website, one that might show up higher in search results than your own website. To make your profile the best that it can be, keep the following tips in mind:

- Create a client-attracting profile summary that clearly identifies how you can help.

- Optimize your profile by including keywords that your clients would use to locate someone who does what you do. For example: If you are a motivational speaker, you might use keywords like: achievement, "being your best", "goal setting", "peak performance", "maximum performance", and "turnaround".

- Create a client-attracting headline. Your profile headline should include your most important keywords and briefly explain what you do and for whom. It can be a powerful "commercial" that follows you everywhere you engage on LinkedIn as it shows up each time you Like,

Share or Comment on someone's content, and each time you post your own content.

- Upload a current professional photo that conveys your brand. Your photo does not have to be professionally taken, but it should be a close up of your face with a plain background – such as a wall. Having a photo helps to build trust by letting everyone know that you are the person attached to the profile. People do business with people that they know, like and trust.

Include pictures, graphics, articles, recommendations, videos, etc., to help your prospects learn more about you and get a better idea of how you can help them.

Outbound Marketing

Once you have built a great profile, it's much easier for prospects to locate you (inbound marketing) and you will feel confident in steering prospects to your profile to learn more about you and your business. Outbound marketing in LinkedIn usually comes in the form of helpful articles, tips, and videos that share information tied to your product or service that is helpful to potential clients. This is referred to as content marketing. To successfully use LinkedIn for outbound marketing, keep these three steps in mind:

Build Your Network

The first step in using LinkedIn as an outbound marketing tool is to build your network. Expanding your network allows you to have access to larger pool of people and allows more people to have access to you. After all, the main purpose of LinkedIn is to connect people. To expand your network:

- Connect with everyone in your personal business database
- Send personalized connection requests to prospects
- Connect with people you've recently met offline and at networking events
- Join LinkedIn Groups that contain your target market
- Connect with influencers and others with large networks
- Use the search feature within LinkedIn to find potential prospects, partners, and influencers
- Ask your connections for introductions to people in their network

Make it a goal to request a specific amount of new connections each week. ALWAYS send personal connection requests rather than clicking on the blue Connect button. Remind people how you met and briefly explain why you want to connect. If trying to connect to someone you do not actually know, review their profile so that you can personalize your request.

Communicate & Engage with Your Network to Build Relationships

Growing your LinkedIn network is important, but that alone will not generate new leads, clients or sales for you. It is imperative that you engage with your connections and prospects to build rapport. This engagement helps to put you on their radar. To engage with your connections:

- Start a conversation after connecting through a private message
- Like, comment, and share posts and articles that are of interest to you and your target market
- Write articles on topics that would be helpful for your target market
- Use the message function in the mobile app to send in instant message to others on line
- Send a voice message through the mobile app
- Send articles, pictures or videos that are of interest through the mobile app

The key to building a following and attracting prospects is to keep all your interactions and your postings in line with your business offerings. Keeping focused on your brand helps prospects understand more about you and your business. Since the invention of the internet, people's buying habits have changed. Buyers are likely to go online to research a product or service before they buy, so it is imperative that you have an online presence that speaks to your product or service and is backed up by recommendations of others. Luckily, LinkedIn is a great tool for showcasing your expertise and also providing social proof by including recommendations from others who have purchased your products or services.

Establishing relationships with your connections is a vital part of your marketing strategy. People buy from people they *know, like* and *trust*, and the best way to gain trust is by showing interest in them. To establish relationships on LinkedIn:

- Show interest in your connections by learning what's important to them – review their profiles
- Pay attention to the content your connections share and engage when relevant
- Engage with those who like, comment and share your content
- Introduce your connections to each other – be a connector
- Participate in your groups by sharing helpful information
- Reply in a timely fashion to any messages that you receive

Find New Prospects

LinkedIn is full of people with whom you can do business. Take an active role in locating prospects by searching for them. There are many ways you can locate new prospects. Following are a few ideas:

- Use the search feature and search filters to find prospects in your own network
- Go deeper with Boolean search – using AND, OR, NOT, quotation marks or parentheses
- Review the connections of your contacts (your 2nd & 3rd level connections)

Start by searching your own network using the search bar and search filters or scrolling through your connection list for ideal prospects. Often, your prospects will be connected to people who will also be good prospects and clients, so be sure to check both your 2nd and 3rd level connections. Also review your connections' network to see if there is an opportunity for an introduction. Having a warm introduction from someone who knows someone you want to meet goes a ways towards making a great connection.

Create your own process by developing scripts that you can use to help move prospects through your sales funnel.

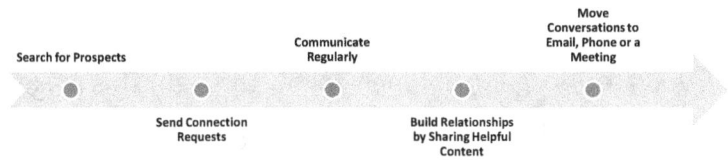

Tips for Building Your Business through LinkedIn

LinkedIn is a goldmine when it comes to business growth. Besides the fact that it is a FREE website and marketing tool, it also provides a perfect way to connect with and keep track of prospects, clients, colleagues, etc. If you are not a daily user of LinkedIn, consider spending at least 15 minutes each day on it. Doing these seven activities daily will help you spread awareness of your business as well as strengthen your network and give you more consistent results.

1. *Check Your LinkedIn Messages Every Day*

   Check LinkedIn every day to catch up on what's new with your connections, respond to messages, and send out messages to people within your network. You must be timely whenever someone reaches out to you.

2. *Grow Your Network*

Invite people you meet at networking events to join your network. Timeliness on this step is important for a couple of reasons.

- You want to ensure that the person you met will remember the meeting or conversation you had with him/her that led to the invitation to join your network.

Taking the first step to send a connection request shows you care and you are very good at timely follow through. This makes a good first impression and suggests that this is how you do all things in your business.

Invite people from their profile page, rather than using a default message, so you can send a personal connection invitation. You only have 300 characters for your message, so include how you met and why you want to connect.

3. *Touch Base in Your Groups*

Review the previous day's emails from group discussions you are following. Join in on conversations to share your expertise.

4. *Review Status Updates/Posts from Your Network*

Review status updates from your network from the previous day. This is your chance to see what your connections think is most important in their lives and then decide what you want to Like, Comment on, or Share. When you share a comment, you are sharing it with all the people in their network and that can be great marketing exposure for you.

5. *Post a Status Update or a Long Post*

   Post a daily update to share information with your entire first-level network and also remind them that you are still out there doing business.

6. *Review Your Notifications*

   Stay connected and top-of-mind with your network by taking advantage of your network's notifications. Congratulate your connections, wish them a happy birthday, or share or comment on their recent post. Make sure to send a personalized message rather than the one provided by LinkedIn.

7. *Review "Who's Viewed Your Profile"*

   Check who has viewed your profile. This LinkedIn feature is a virtual goldmine. If people have looked at your profile and they look interesting to you, don't hesitate to connect with them or send them a message if you're already connected. They have taken the first step—they looked at you. Now it's your move.

The entire business world has gone digital. LinkedIn is the one digital platform that can help you reach your next client quickly. People on LinkedIn are there to do business. With just a little bit of research and promotion, your business can attract top clients. LinkedIn is the one platform that provides detailed information about you and your business as well as your prospects. It's easy, free and at your fingertips – so take advantage of it. Your prospects are on LinkedIn!

Cheryl Matt

In addition to working one-on-one with business owners to create an "Operational Blueprint", Cheryl also speaks and conducts seminars and workshops on a variety of topics including:

- Using LinkedIn for Business Growth
- Getting More Done in Less Time
- Strategic Planning is NOT Optional for Small Businesses
- Why Businesses Must Have Systems/Routines for Everything

Contact Info:

Website: CBMBusinessConsulting.com

Email: Cheryl@CBMBusinessConsulting.com

Phone: (804) 467-1179

LinkedIn: Cheryl Matt

Live Life with Intention

Teri Karjala

Whether we believe it or not, we are all very powerful and potent beings. However, our potency is only as strong as we allow it to be.

There is one common **thread** woven into the fabric of human life and that is the underlying need to create abundance, to create *more.*

More may look different **to** each individual, but at the end of the day, we all want to create *more* in order to lead a rich, fulfilling life where the greatest amount of joy can be experienced.

But how can we create **more** in our lives with a lot less effort?

Here are three easy ways:

1. Be open to receiving
2. Set intentions
3. Ask generative questions

Working with female entrepreneurs, I see a great imbalance in our give / receive ratio. We often give quite generously as compared to our ability **to** receive in return. However, in order to create *more* for ourselves, we must be able to <u>receive</u>.

I'm not suggesting we stop giving, for giving provides us with countless benefits. **By** giving *and* receiving, we allow the energy of the universe to stay in motion. But giving without receiving is futile for creating *more* in our lives, and it is the act of receiving that allows our desires to come to fruition.

So how do we put our **newfound** skill of receiving into motion to create *more*? This is where the practice of setting intentions plays an important role. When activated, intentions set our desired outcomes in motion.

The definition of the word **intention**, in fact, is "an aim that guides action." Setting intentions makes a request and is the first step in generating the *more* we so desire. It gives us the opportunity to alter our circumstances and impact our world.

Start each day by setting intentions by answering a simple question: *Where do I desire to go*? Or, *What do I desire to have?* Set the intention for **what** you would like to receive. Write your daily intentions in a journal, on a notepad, or in your Daily Intentions Planner, a tool I crafted to map out intentions and make note of the changes they manifest.

One of my coaching clients, Stephanie, began setting daily intentions after learning the practice in my workshop. She happened to be using my Daily Intentions Planner to guide her so she could clearly see her results. Within one week, not only did she experience tremendous shifts in her life, but she was also able to create *more*. For her, *more* was bringing an additional $8,000 of revenue into her business, as if by magic.

Setting intentions isn't unique to me. Oprah often speaks about setting intentions and how doing so directly contributed to her success. If Oprah can reap the benefits of setting intentions, so can we!

Finally, to generate your *more* with a lot less effort, ask the universe generative questions. One question I like to ask is: *"What contribution can I be and receive today?"* I ask this question three times, without answering it, and it allows me to remain open to all possibilities. This is really quite juicy as I can't even begin to fathom what the universe has in store for me. Ask this question excessively to see magnificent results manifest in your life. It's a very powerful tool.

I give you permission to play in a place where possibilities abound, to find balance between giving and receiving, embrace a daily intention-setting practice, and ask the universe generative questions that lead to the *more* you have always dreamed of.

Talking with Teri's Famous *Daily Intentions Planner*

I created the *Daily Intentions Planner* to keep me focused and on track to success. In the past, my attention and focus were scattered around. I'm a high energy person, which is often a gift, but sometimes a curse when it comes to taking inspired action, reaching my targets, and creating *more* in my life.

The planner started as a tool I just used personally, but then my friends and colleagues wanted one...and their friends and colleges asked for one...and so on, until it made sense to make the planner available to the public.

The *Daily Intentions Planner* is a guided daily journal designed to help you set your daily intentions, track short-term targets that keep you on the path to reaching your long-term targets, follow your progress, note the results, and remain grateful along the way. It's a tool you'll be grateful to have as you embark on creating the life of your dreams.

Teri Karjala

Teri Karjala is owner and founder of Creative Counseling Center, LLC and Talking **With** Teri. She is the author of the best-selling book, *Be the Magic of You: Tools to Transform Your Life*, with the foreword written by Jack Canfield, author of the *Chicken Soup for the Soul* series. Teri is a teacher, trainer, international keynote speaker, and has been featured in interviews on various TV, radio, and podcast shows.

Today, women entrepreneurs hire her to ignite the magic within. Most come to Teri consumed by fear, beat down by unconscious limiting beliefs, are addicted to self-sabotage... and lack the tools to get back on track. Teri helps them unleash their greatest transformation by releasing the blocks that hold them back personally and professionally, to catapult their business, generate more money, more clients, and more freedom, with a lot less effort.

Outside of the office, Teri spends her time with family and friends. Teri loves playing outdoors, crafting and creating, doodling, and participating in any thrill-seeking adventure!

Contact Info:

Teri is available to support you on your journey. Let her know how she can help by contacting her through her website at www.talkingwithteri.com.

To buy Teri's *Daily Intentions Planner,* go to www.talkingwithteri.com/stop-shop/.

Phone: (303) 843-6000

The Mission-Driven Entrepreneur
Dr. Shantell Malachi

In early 2011, I was a burnt out and overwhelmed human resource executive/part-time serial entrepreneur looking for a little more passion in my professional life. I had spent the better half of the previous ten years helping small businesses get started in my role as a consultant, had grown a successful mental health practice, and was leading the human resources (HR) department at one of the nation's oldest Historically Black Colleges and Universities. Unfortunately, that just wasn't enough. My childhood was not full of wealth or even happiness. I was all too familiar with what philanthropy experts would call the most downtrodden segments of our society. Because of this, my sole purpose in life was to be happy and at peace. When my career began to get in the way of my purpose, I knew I had to make a change.

When my HR career grew, I used every opportunity to share my knowledge and expertise with members of my community who might not otherwise have had access to a coach or consultant. Sitting in my office one day, after eight hours of continuous meetings (that could have been accomplished in four short emails), I Googled "organizations that help women find jobs" and came across Dress for Success Worldwide. I had heard the cliché "dress for success" several times over in my career, and I vaguely remembered a past co-worker collecting clothes for Dress for Success. However, what I saw on their website that day was so much more. I was in complete awe of this amazing organization that provides professional clothing, learning opportunities, and emotional support for women reentering the workforce. I had to learn more!

I contacted the local number listed and left a message. After a few days of not receiving a response, I did a little more digging and came across the number for Dress for Success' headquarters in New York. I called the number and spoke to an amazingly friendly young lady named Lexi. I told her that I had contacted my local affiliate but hadn't been able to reach anyone. She informed me that the local office had closed some time ago and that Dress for Success was not servicing clients in my area at the time. She said Dress for Success had no intentions of returning to the Central Virginia market. I was completely heartbroken.

From that point, a three-hour conversation ensued about the history of Dress for Success, their amazing business model, and how they were helping hundreds of thousands of women around the world achieve economic independence through their workforce development programs. I was completely blown away but was totally disappointed that I wouldn't be able to volunteer for this awesome organization locally. Then Lexi said the words that changed my career trajectory: "Why don't you consider starting an affiliate?" At first, I was taken aback. Me? Start a nonprofit? I had no real nonprofit experience outside of volunteering for my local church and a few mentoring programs. Never one to back down from a challenge, however, I told her to send me the information for new affiliates and I would think it over.

Over the next few days, Dress for Success didn't leave my mind. I thought constantly about how I could help so many women gain their footing in the workforce using my skills as a human resource professional, but I worried that I didn't have the knowledge to start a nonprofit. I did my research. I asked questions. I prayed. Finally, I took action. I put out a call to action to women in my network and began drafting a business plan.

Although Dress for Success is an international brand, starting an affiliate is much like starting any other organization from scratch. Each Dress for Success affiliate (currently there are 153 and counting) is independently led and operated. Legal documents, tax exemption, governing boards, and the like can be intimidating. I would be lying if I said it was easy.

Fast forward seven years and I'm proud to say that Dress for Success Central Virginia is a thriving nonprofit organization with accolades and awards to boot. We have served thousands of women, raised hundreds of thousands of dollars, made a measurable impact in the local community, and are improving or implementing programs regularly. This journey has not been easy but has certainly been worth it.

I have learned so much about building and growing nonprofits. I am afforded opportunities to evolve on a personal and professional level through my work with Dress for Success and other nonprofit organizations. Since founding Dress for Success Central Virginia, my consulting practice has evolved to serve emerging nonprofits. Through customer-focused consulting, training, and customized coaching, my practice called Nonprofitability™ generates creative solutions that strengthen the excellence of individuals and organizations dedicated to empowering their communities. I've spoken on national stages and now teach the principles that I've learned at the collegiate level.

Starting a nonprofit has been one of the most rewarding ventures of my life. While running a nonprofit isn't for everyone, I encourage everyone to make charity a part of their work. Give a percentage of your profit to a cause about which you're passionate, start a mentoring program for your industry, or donate your excess inventory to a local shelter. You'll find that adding a philanthropic flair to your life makes for a much more meaningful, purposeful path.

Dr. Shantell J. Malachi, PhD
Accomplished Serial Entrepreneur,
Business Strategist, Philanthropist
Dress for Success

As an entrepreneur, Dr. Shantell J. Malachi, PhD has developed an impressive business portfolio that includes ventures in healthcare, the nonprofit sector, consulting, media, and cultural arts. A true student of organizational development, Shantell has matched extensive education and training with over 15 years of experience as a coach and consultant to create methods that help businesses launch, grow, and maximize their profit.

Always keeping community engagement and outreach at the forefront of her work, Shantell founded and currently serves as the Executive Director of Dress for Success® Central Virginia, a Richmond, Virginia, based affiliate of the international nonprofit organization that promotes the economic independence of disadvantaged women by providing professional attire, a network of support, and the career development tools to help women thrive in work and in life. Dress for Success Central Virginia helps more than 200 women annually move towards self-sufficiency through its Suiting Program, Career Center, and Professional Women's Group. In addition to leading Dress for Success Central Virginia, Shantell currently sits on the YWCA of Richmond Young Professionals Board as well as the Board of Directors for Children Incorporated where she is the Vice Chairperson. Shantell is a graduate of Nonprofit Learning Point's Emerging Nonprofit Leader program and a fellow to Virginia Commonwealth University's Division of Community Engagement.

For her business acumen and nonprofit work, Shantell has been recognized by countless organizations including Omega Psi Phi Fraternity Inc., Yahoo! Women Who Shine, Style Weekly Magazine (2012 Top 40 Under 40 Award Recipient), Belle Magazine, and The Richmond Free Press.

Shantell received her Bachelor of Science in Business Administration from Virginia Commonwealth University, her Master of Business Administration from Strayer University, and her PhD in Organizational Management from Capella University all with specializations in Human Resource Management.

Contact Info:

Website: centralvirginia.dressforsuccess.org

Email: shantell@dfscentralvirginia.org

Office phone: (804) 234-3034

Facebook: www.facebook.com/DressForSuccessCVA

Twitter: @DFSCentralVA

Instagram: @dfscentralva

The mission of Dress for Success is to empower women to achieve economic independence by providing a network of support, professional attire and the development tools to help women thrive in work and in life.

Budgeting Tips for the Unbudgetable
Sorana Blackfoot

After living in the world of the known (and quite small) paycheck for a number of years, and then being self-employed for another number of years, I learned that I liked writing my own paycheck better. I also learned that there are risks with this choice, and I have friends in my life who still cannot understand my choice, even after more than ten years. One thing is for sure: it is not for the faint at heart – and you need to know yourself, your business, and your finances very well if you want to be successful.

During my years of serving women who work for themselves, either as business owners or as self-employed, I learned that many of them went into the business because of their passion for what they do, their desire for independence, or even sometimes because of their circumstances. While all these are valid reasons and by no means obstacles to building a successful business, the one thing that stands out for me is the lack of business knowledge for many women I meet. And I mean all the parts of their business that are not directly related with the object of their business (a.k.a. their passion).

The geeky part of my brain became fascinated with deciphering the strategies that can increase the profitability of the business, regardless of the field or industry. My main focus has been for years in the financial field, therefore the cashflow and the increase of the bottom line became my main area of interest in business.

Since moving to the United States in 2002, I had to learn a new financial system and way of handling money. In my native country of Romania, I never even knew of or saw a credit card, and never heard of a credit score or history. I became first intrigued, then fascinated, and ultimately savvy in the way the money flows between people (often escaping through their fingers). To my shock, I realized that I wasn't the only one who needed to learn all this information, and then decided to share my knowledge focusing mainly on women for two main reasons: I can relate with them (duh!), and I discovered that the woman can influence the situation of the entire family – for better or for worse.

In my position as investment adviser, my main goal is to set up systems so my clients can generate the money that will permit them to retire at the age they desire while also living the lifestyle of their dreams. While this sounds great in theory, I learned through the years that many of my prospects had big dreams (which is great) but little discipline or probability to accomplish those dreams with the knowledge they had. I decided to do something about it, something more than simply looking for other clients.

While sitting down with a client, my main goal is to give them a clear picture of their financial situation first, and then find out where they want to be and when, from a financial standpoint. The rest, while not easy, is simple: figure out how to get from where they are to where they want to be, and if at all possible, in the time they want to allocate to this journey.

I am aware that many women business owners reading these lines will think that they may not be able to get it done alone, or they may feel overwhelmed by the fact that their financial situation is not what they want it to be. Even though this may seem very tough, it is definitely not an unsurmountable obstacle. The easiest way to jump over such obstacle is by finding a partner that gives you a hand in climbing over it, a.k.a. a financial professional that can design your plan. Most people thinking about the plan for improving their financial situation through organizing their money in a more efficient way, are intimidated by the process they have always heard called a BUDGET.

Sitting down with someone who can help you organize your cash flow in such a way as to maximize your financial results can be intimidating at first but ultimately is freeing. Most such professionals may be used to working with employees who have a constant cash flow in the form of weekly, biweekly, or monthly paychecks. As a business owner or self-employed person, this may seem irrelevant or even scary, since regular income may be a challenge, especially in the beginning of the entrepreneurial journey.

I have been self-employed and a business owner for more than fourteen years, so I can understand the fears and doubts that come with the fluctuating income. As I work with other people who also have the inconsistent cash flow, I have come up with seven tips on setting up a budget for an unbudgetable situation.

TIP 1. Track your habits first – for two to three months, so you don't get a false image. The month you are tracking may not show things the way they usually are. You can even use a notebook if technology is a challenge, or you can use a computer program if you like technology. All you need to do is track the money you have coming in every month and also the expenses you have. If you really want a true picture, you need to track EVERYTHING. If you don't have the patience to track every penny, make an effort for two to three months; keep yourself motivated by knowing this will only be for a set period of time.

TIP 2. Categorize your expenses into three categories: fixed, flexible, and discretionary.

Fixed expenses include: mortgage/rent, car payment, insurances, utilities, debt payments, and memberships in professional organizations, etc.;

Flexible expenses include: gas for your car or public transportation, groceries, charity contributions, and work/business-related travel expenses, etc.;

Discretionary expenses include: eating out, entertainment, hobbies, clothes, and shoes, etc.

One very important thing to remember is that some of the fixed expenses can be reduced or renegotiated. The monthly expense will be lowered but it will still be a fixed amount afterwards. An example of such a case is a mortgage that is refinanced, or a phone bill that is changed based on need (changing phone plan or changing phone company).

When making sure all expenses are covered, your money is directed first towards the fixed expenses, then the flexible ones, and only what is left can be used for discretionary expenses. As you analyze where your money is going, you can also look into reducing some of the expenses by changing the frequency of some of the services you use, or limiting the travel. Even though these expenses may fit into the fixed or flexible categories, they can still be reduced.

TIP 3. Save money on things you no longer use. For example, some of the professional memberships and subscriptions you signed up for may not be needed or of interest anymore. You can reduce your expenses by cancelling some of the monthly payments you make to them. This money can then be redirected into savings and/or investments. If you are a member of various professional organizations, you need to ensure there is a return for your investment in order to keep the membership.

TIP 4. Direct money from your checking account into savings on a regular basis. Start with a negligible amount that you won't miss and set up a monthly transfer to another account. You can increase that amount every month or every few months as you wish. This can be also a percentage of the money you receive from a regular client. It is preferable that you set it up to happen automatically and don't have to do this each time you receive a check from a client. This money should move over without you seeing it in your checking account because you may be tempted to find other uses for it besides saving it.

TIP 5. Pay yourself first from each check you receive. As a business owner or commission earner, your checks will vary from month to month, from one client to another. The best way to set up this system is by percentage, instead of a set amount (this is better for employees who receive a regular paycheck). This payment that you make to yourself should be saved for your future. As a business owner, it will be part of your exit strategy. It should go towards long-term investments and retirement.

TIP 6. Set up a "Justin" Account – your emergency fund. A percentage from each check you receive needs to go into an account that you can easily access and remain there until you accumulate enough to cover all your fixed and flexible expenses for at least a couple of months. You can also set a goal of a certain amount, like $3000, $5000, or what you may need to spend on an unexpected but unavoidable bill, such as car repairs, or fixing a major appliance in your home or business.

I like to use the name "Justin" Account instead of Emergency Fund because of the bad energy the word emergency carries. "Justin" Account stands for "just in case" something happens. You are not giving money to anyone named Justin.

TIP 7. Protect yourself and your family with insurance. Talk to a professional. As a responsible business owner and family pillar, you need to ensure that your family is protected in case something happens to you. You should talk to an insurance professional and analyze your need for life insurance, disability insurance, and liability insurance for your business and home, etc.

These are some quick tips for you to start figuring out where your money is going. It is not a be-all end-all recipe for budgeting. I wrote this chapter to help you as the busy business women take a look at their cash flow and make some adjustments that can put them closer to their financial goals. I also believe that we all have to continuously work on bringing in more money and then focus on keep more of the money we make. As your business grows, you also have to keep an eye on where your money is going once you get it, not solely on making more money; if you have leaks, your bottom line still doesn't get to the level you want. Many accountants will advise you on how to lower your taxes; yes, business expenses are tax deductible, but make sure you don't spend money for the sake of a business deduction.

May this information prove useful for improving your financial IQ. May it serve you to build your financial serenity!

Sorana Blackfoot
Prosperity Mentor
Un-Broke Women

Women too often find themselves in a precarious situation, alone, and uncomfortable dealing with money due to divorce or widowhood. Sorana Blackfoot's great passion as a Prosperity Mentor is teaching women to create, preserve, and transfer their wealth. Sorana's clients gain control of their investments and become confident, supported, and financially secure. With over a decade of financial career experience, Sorana personally coaches all of her clients through her company, Un-Broke Women, by advising them on building better relationships with their money.

In 2002, Sorana uprooted from Romania in order built a successful career in the financial industry in the United States. Sorana discloses her life story and the money lessons she learned living on two continents and through three different regimes in her Amazon best-selling book, "New World, New Dreams: My Money Story," which was published in January 2018.

As part of her ongoing mission to empower women to achieve financial serenity, Sorana founded the Business Resources for Inspiring Leaders Conference, or BRIL Conference. An annual business conference for women launched in Richmond, Virginia, in 2018 and held every March, the goal of the BRIL Conference is to empower women to design an inspiring business and positively impact their community.

Contact Info:

Website: www.unbrokewomen.com and
            www.brilconference.com

Email: sorana@unbrokewomen.com

Phone: (804) 687-2384

Facebook: www.facebook.com/financialmakeovers
www.facebook.com/brilconference

Blogs Are Beautiful! Five Powerful Ways Blogs Improve Your Business

Kim Eley

"But I'm not a writer!"

I hear it all the time. When I tell entrepreneurs that they should be writing a blog, I get more pushback to that idea than a kid parked in front of a bowl of mushy Brussel sprouts.

And I get it! As an entrepreneur I used to think to myself, "I'm crazy busy. I don't have time to write a blog!"

But I've learned that **blogs are powerful**! They enable you to connect with your clients on a more meaningful level, which means you can share more about you and your business in an efficient way.

Entrepreneurs should embrace these online articles of awesomeness. That's why I'm going to reveal five reasons why blogs are beautiful!

First, blogs let your clients (and potential clients) get to know you better.

People want to work with people they know, like, and trust, according to Ivan Meisner, founder of the business networking group, BNI. Say you have been connected to a potential client, and they are interested in your business. But first, they want to know more about you. Sure, they can look at your social media posts and your website to find out about your business. You have likely carefully crafted messages that explain exactly what you provide to your clients. But do they tell anything about YOU?

An interested client certainly wants your services or they wouldn't be looking at your social media and your site. To most clients, it is not just your services that they are interested in. They want to know what it would be like to work with you. What are you like as a service provider?

One great way to let your client know who you are, what makes you tick, and what you're passionate about is through blogs on your website. Your blogs are windows of insight you construct through text and photos. They tell the client what you do, but more importantly, they let the client know who you are.

Let your potential client know:

- Your "Origin Story!" How did you start your business? Tell your story about why you started your business. What fuels your passion to do what you do? Dedicate a blog post or two about what made you want to create your biz.

- Behind the Curtain – You've got a busy business life! People are always interested to know what goes into running a business and how it works. Let your clients see "behind the curtain" of your everyday life. If you have a physical product, show the decisions you make to design your labels, for example. If you offer services, let customers see how you interact with your clients. Do a Facebook live when you have a client meeting! Then record that video and include it as a blog post. Show the behind-the-scenes if you film a promotional video. And be authentically you!

- Details they didn't know. Isn't it fun to learn something that's not well known? As a publisher, people are always asking me questions about the writing process. I like to write blogs that talk about the steps you need to take to write a book. Blogs like these give you a chance to share interesting facts to educate and entertain your potential client. Plus your clients will get a kick out of being featured as one of your VIPs!

Second, blogs encourage customer engagement.

Your potential client is looking at your blog. How will you engage them once they are there?

This is the cool part. It's your platform! Your blog is like your blank canvas for your words and pictures to express yourself and connect with your client. With your blog, you can provide content to your clients that they will love, and they will want to keep coming back to you for more!

Some ways you can do this include:

- Tutorials – Knowledge is power, right? Empower your client by teaching them about your services. What is it you would like for them to know about what you do? SHARE IT ON YOUR BLOG!

- News About You! Your blog is a great way to get the word on to your clients about what's fresh and new in your world! Do you have a new product? Introduce it in your blog!

- Customer stories - Would you like to celebrate one of your client's successes? Write it on your blog! Word of caution – make sure to respect industry regulations before sharing as some industries do not allow you to share client information. Also, no matter what field you are in, it is professional courtesy to ask for permission from your client before sharing their information, even positive information such as a success.

- Professional or personal resource – Do you know someone who is in a similar field to you? You can use a blog to interview them and have your clients get to know them. You can also include a testimonial. Why not? It's your blog! Share your success stories!

Blogs are more than just writing! You can also post in different ways: audio and visual in addition to writing. Why? People like to be communicated with in different ways.

- Videos are especially engaging to your audience. Consider adding video content to your blog. According to Wordstream:[1]
  - 82% of Twitter users watch video content on Twitter
  - YouTube has over a billion users, almost one-third of total internet users.
  - 45% of people watch more than an hour of Facebook or YouTube videos a week.
  - More than 500 million hours of videos are watched on YouTube each day.
  - More video content is uploaded in 30 days than the major U.S. television networks have created in 30 years.
  - 87% of online marketers use video content.
- Audio is another powerful way to share your message. A podcast is a way to share an audio "blog" with your audience. As an audio blogger, your content:[2]
  - Is easier to consume by your audience.
  - Can be monetized effectively.
  - Can be listened to just about anywhere.
  - Can reach a new audience that doesn't read blog posts.

Third, strategic blogs + social media = TRAFFIC!

---

[1] https://www.wordstream.com/blog/ws/2017/03/08/video-marketing-statistics
[2] https://blogging.com/podcasting/

Like two partners working together for you, blogs and social media work together to bring you traffic from clients. How?

Talk in person to others at networking events. Go out and be social! While you are out and about, identify events and influencers at the events that you can utilize to promote your post.

For example, say you have been invited to a large conference with other vendors, potential clients, and other awesome participants. After the event, write a great blog about it. Make sure to write about how you and your business were involved. Then post your blog post on Facebook and tag your peers, other vendors, and participants. Make it super fun! You'll likely find that many will share your post! And this will drive more traffic to your blog to find out more.

Fourth, you can repurpose the content!

Blog posts are like a treasure trove of content. Write once, share many times! When you write a story about your business in a blog, you can use excerpts from your blog for:

- Instagram – Since Instagram is all about pictures, why not share an intriguing photo along with a link to your blog? Also, on your Instagram profile, add a link to your blog on your website.
- Facebook – When you add a post on Facebook, add something about your blog post. Then paste the URL to your blog under your text. The photo of your blog post will appear as a part of your post. Once the blog post snippet appears, delete the link you added. The blog URL will remain and the snippet will still be shown under your text. Use the "Post" button to post your blog link to

Facebook. [3]And there you have it! Additional exposure to your awesome blog!

- Twitter – Sharing your blog posts on Twitter is a fantastic way to get more traffic on your blog by tweeting a link to each new post you write.
- LinkedIn – Whenever you write a new blog, be sure to copy and share the link to your blog on LinkedIn. Also, include a link to your blog in your LinkedIn profile, making it easy for your connections and people interested in you to find your blogs.

Do you conduct workshops? Your blog content can be used as the start of training you can share with people either in person in a classroom or online in a webinar. In addition, you can choose topics for your workshops based on which of your blogs receive the most feedback. In this way, your blogs are a great marketing tool to find out which topics are most valued by your clients. This is great to know when you prepare workshops and other informational products that you can monetize.

Fifth, you can put your content together to write a book!

Have you wanted to write a book but were intimidated by the amount of work it might take? Blogs to the rescue! By writing blogs a week or month at a time, you have already started creating your chapters for your book. Just as you can repurpose your blogs into social media posts, you can also craft your blog posts into your amazing book.

Start blogging today! As your clients get to know the real you, your business will increase. That's worth blogging about!

---

[3] https://www.lifewire.com/add-blog-to-facebook-profile-3476684

Kim Eley
CEO, Writing Coach and Publisher
KWE Publishing

Kim, an author, a writing coach, a publisher, and a speaker, is best known for snorting when she laughs. She is the founder and CEO of KWE Publishing LLC, a publishing company whose mission is to bring magic to writers to go from idea to printed book! She's assisted lots of writers to become authors and publish their incredible messages. Her own book, "Tickers! What Makes People...Tick! And Pursue a Career They Love," spotlights incredible entrepreneurs and business people who were relentless in pursuing their dream career. She published her book in 2016 and since that time, has helped numerous writers to become authors.

Her 20 plus years of technical writing, project management, and life coaching skills combined with a fun and playful approach to work make Kim an outstanding publisher who gets results. She holds a Bachelor's degree in English from the College of William & Mary and a Master's degree in Writing & Rhetoric from Virginia Commonwealth University. Kim also completed coursework as a Martha Beck Wayfinder Life Coach in 2017.

Kim is from Virginia. She is happily married to her BFF. Kim adores cats, orchids, cooking for friends and family, and gets all her news from comedy channels.

Contact Info:

Website: www.kwepub.com

Email: kwe@kwepub.com

Phone: 804-536-1972

Unarmed But Dangerous
Tawana Williams

Tawana Williams, a speaker, author, artist, advocate, TV personality, businesswoman, executive producer, co-producer, humanitarian and CEO of Tawana Williams Outreach, Inc., was born without arms and has impaired use of her legs due to the drug Thalidomide that was given to her mother during pregnancy.

Tawana has a powerful and uplifting message for all generations. Her compelling story is one of triumph, perseverance and determination. Tawana has overcome many obstacles; she was gang raped during a home invasion, raped by her step father, addicted to crack and cocaine for 10 years; she's also experienced abortion, motherhood, a stroke, and a mild heart attack; she's never let her challenges or disability stop her. Tawana has many gifts and accomplishments.

She's an internationally known Les Brown Platinum Motivational Speaker, Author, Artist, Advocate, TV Personality, Businesswoman, Executive Producer, Co-Producer, Humanitarian and CEO of Tawana Williams Outreach, Inc. She became a professional speaker in 1996. Tawana is the author of six books, including her classic book "UNarmed But Dangerous: The Tawana Williams Story"; this is her true-life story of 'heroism' which will be featured as her debut movie "Eagle Without Wings" in theaters coming soon.

Tawana was a guest on The Jerry Springer Show, sharing her story of how she beat the odds; she was invited to The Judge

Hatchett Show, as a mentor to a troubled teen. In addition, she has appeared on The WORD Network, Manna Express TV, TCT-Alive, TCT-Rejoice, TCT-Ask The Pastor, TCT-Triangle Alive, Atlanta Live, Lifetime TV, The 700 Club/CBN, TBN Network, "Your World" with Creflo Dollar, and many other regional and national programs. She's had phone interviews twice with Oprah's Producers. In 2007, Tawana and her husband Toby were featured in *Homes of Color Magazine*, *Hope for Women Magazine* and *Epitome Magazine*, just to name a few.

Tawana produced her own radio show that was syndicated in more than a million households in Memphis and Nashville, Tennessee. In March 2008, she was the recipient of The True Servant Award from the Agape Gospel Academy Awards Ceremony. Tawana has countless awards, accolades, appearances, certificates and newspaper articles. She's the former Spokesperson for The Agape Gospel Academy in Atlanta, Georgia from 2008-2011.

She was the Special Guest for world-renowned motivational speaker, Mr. Les Brown, at the Speakers Network Training in Atlanta, Georgia. While there, she captured the minds and hearts of other professional speakers. She's been a Les Brown Platinum Motivational Speaker since 2004.

Tawana is currently lobbying Congress for Family Assistance Rest Rooms (F.A.R.R.) in all airports throughout America.
You can read and sign her petition @
www.TawanaWilliams.com.

Tawana Williams is "The Hope Coach." Her dreams are to create and host her own talk show, motivational reality show, to executive produce her documentary and co-produce her debut movie, "Eagle Without Wings," and to perform humanitarian efforts to help people around the globe.

Contact Info:

Tawana and her husband, Toby, reside in Wilson, North Carolina. Her book, "UNarmed But Dangerous," her other books, artwork, DVDs and products are available exclusively @ www.TawanaWilliams.com.

To know more about her upcoming debut movie, to become an executive producer, and to see your name on the credits, on the IMDB website, and to have a reserved seat at the Red-Carpet Epic Gala, or to be called as an extra, and other perks in "Eagle Without Wings," please visit www.EagleWithoutWings.com or call (252) 291-6081.

Bibliography

The New Psychology of Marketing

Cialdini, Robert. *Influence: The Psychology of Persuasio*n, Harper Business; Revised Edition, December 26, 2006.

Corliss, Rebecca. *LinkedIn 277% More Effective for Lead Generation Than Facebook & Twitter [New Data],* January 30, 2012. https://blog.hubspot.com/blog/tabid/6307/bid/30030/linkedin-277-more-effective-for-lead-generation-than-facebook-twitter-new-data.aspx

Leveraging LinkedIn For Business Growth

Rynne, Alex, *10 Surprising Stats You Didn't Know about Marketing on LinkedIn [Infographic],* February 1, 2017. https://business.linkedin.com/marketing-solutions/blog/linkedin-b2b-marketing/2017/10-surprising-stats-you-didnt-know-about-marketing-on-linkedin

Blogs Are Beautiful!

Misner, Ivan, "The Three Phases of Networking: The VCP Process®", https://ivanmisner.com/category/credibility/

Lister, Mary. "37 Staggering Video Marketing Statistics for 2018", **January 24, 2019,** https://www.wordstream.com/blog/ws/2017/03/08/video-marketing-statistics.

Yates, Laura. Starting Your First Podcast In 2019 The Easy Way, May 16, 2018, https://blogging.com/podcasting/.

Leaders Are Readers

Our authors recommend these titles:

The Entrepreneur's Solution: The Modern Millionaire's Path to More Profit, Fans & Freedom, Mel H. Abraham

Finding Your Own North Star: Claiming the Life You Were Meant to Live, Martha Beck

Who Moved My Cheese?: An A-Mazing Way to Deal with Change in Your Work and in Your Life, Kenneth Blanchard and Spencer Johnson

Dare to Lead: Brave Work. Tough Conversations. Whole Hearts, Brené Brown

Influence: The Psychology of Persuasion, Robert B. Cialdini, Ph.D.

Getting to Yes: Negotiating Agreement without Giving In, Roger Fisher and William L. Ury

Purple Cow: Transform Your Business By Being Remarkable, Seth Godin

The Big Leap: Conquer Your Hidden Fear and Take Life to the Next Level, Gay Hendricks

How the World Sees You: Discover Your Highest Value Through the Science of Fascination, Sally Hogshead

The Code of the Extraordinary Mind: 10 Unconventional Laws to Redefine Your Life and Succeed On Your Own Terms, Vishen Lakhiani

Essentialism: The Disciplined Pursuit of Less, Greg McKeown

The Pumpkin Plan: A Simple Strategy to Grow a Remarkable Business in Any Field, Mike Michalowicz

Failing Forward: Turning Mistakes into Stepping Stones for Success, John C. Maxwell

Battlefield of the Mind: Winning the Battle in Your Mind, Joyce Meyer

Profit First: Transform Your Business from a Cash-Eating Monster to a Money-Making Machine, Michael Michalowicz

The 12 Week Year: Get More Done in 12 Weeks than Others Do in 12 Months, Brian P. Moran and Michael Lennington

The Power of Your Subconscious Mind, Dr. Joseph Murphy

Money, A Love Story: Untangle Your Financial Woes and Create the Life You Really Want, Kate Northrup

The Art of Living, Bob Proctor and Sandra Gallagher

You Are a Badass®: How to Stop Doubting Your Greatness and Start Living an Awesome Life, Jen Sincero

You Are What You Believe: Simple Steps to Transform Your Life, Hyrum W. Smith and Ken Blanchard

A New Earth: Awakening to Your Life's Purpose, Eckhart Tolle

The Art of War, Sun Tzu

On Writing Well, William Zinsser